THE REALM OF DECLARATORY GRACE

Workbook

CATRINA J. SPARKMAN
THE IRONER'S PRESS

Copyright © 2023 Catrina J. Sparkman

Published by:

The Ironer's Press

1102 Engelhart Drive

Madison, WI 53713

All rights reserved. No part of this book may be reproduced, stored in whole or in part or transmitted in any form by any means, without prior written permission from the publisher, except in the case of brief quotations embodied in articles for review. Nor can this book be circulated in any form of binding or cover other than that in which it is published.

This is a work of fiction. Any reference or similarities to actual events, real people, living or dead, or to real locales are intended to give the novel a sense of reality. Any similarity in other names, characters, places and incidents is entirely coincidental.

Contents

Author's Note	V
Introduction	X
DECLARATORY GRACE OILS	XXI
1. THE OIL OF LIVE	1
My Decree to Live	6
2. THE OIL OF STAND	7
My Decree to Stand	13
3. THE OIL OF REMEMBER	14
My Decree to Remember	20
4. THE OIL OF THRIVE	21
My Decree to Thrive	28
5. THE OIL OF LAUGHTER	29

My Decree to Laugh	36
6. THE OIL OF RETURN	37
My Decree to Return	44
7. THE OIL OF KEEP	45
My Decree to Keep	50
8. THE OIL OF RELEASE	51
My Decree to Release	57
9. THE OIL OF EXPECT	58
My Decree to Expect	63
10. THE OIL OF CREATE	64
My Personal Declaration	72
11. APPENDIX A	73
12. APPENDIX B	79
About Author	95
Also By	97

Author's Note

Welcome Dear Reader,

to *The Realm of Declaratory Grace Workbook*. This is the seventh book in a series of books called *Doing Business with God*. The purpose of this series is to present timely kingdom concepts in an easily digestible format. You can read most of the books in the Doing Business with God series in one or two sittings. They are designed to be consumed quickly because I want the concepts presented in those books to catch fire in your belly. I want you to glean the knowledge within the pages quickly so that you can go forth and *be* God's kingdom. I wrote this book to be a companion guide to my Declaratory Grace Anointing Oil line. The oils in the Declaratory Grace line are made from a thoughtful blend of essential oils mixed in virgin olive oil. Each unique blend is one that I believe our Heavenly Father has given me. You will see that there are ten oils in this line, and they are listed by chapter in this book in the order in which they should be experienced. Each chapter bears the name of a different oil. If you take a quick peek at the table of contents, you will see some random looking words are listed in parentheses after the name of each oil. These words are not random, they represent the biblical meaning behind the oils given number. For example, one is a number in the Bible that represents Unity. As you anoint yourself with the oil of Live, I pray that you come into unity in your mind and in your heart with the destiny that God has in store for your life. Stand is the second oil in the line that you should use. For the oil of Stand, I want you to come into divine fellowship with the people God has placed you in fellowship with; so that you can be a witness in the earth of what a follower of Christ is truly supposed to be. I also want you to fall out of agreement with people who mean you no good. I also want you to fall out of agreement with demonic powers that come to destroy the unity between brethren. Wouldn't you know it, two is a number in the Bible that represents Union, Division, and Witness?

THE REALM OF DECLARATORY GRACE

Now, all that being said, I expect this book to go around the entire world. If you are reading this book or hearing, it read in your presence if that be the case, I want you to declare whether you use my oils or not. There is tremendous power in agreeing with what the God of the multiverse has to say about you and then changing your words to match His heart. So, if you don't have access to the oils in my line, use whatever you have on hand. Even if all you have is water. And, if you live in a region of the world where water is too precious of a commodity, use dirt. Yeah, I said it. Bless the dirt in the name of Jesus. Anoint yourself with it as a prophetic act. Start declaring and keep it moving.

If you are reading or listening to this book, you will see that I have included an anchoring scripture verse or passage for each oil in my line. Information on the therapeutic qualities of the oils used in my blends, a personal message from Father God to you, and a daily declaration that you can say aloud as you anoint yourself. Think of this book as your training ground. Every Friday morning for the past 18 years, from 3 to 6

AM CST, I have led and trained an intercessory prayer group called the 4th Watch. This prayer group is open to anyone in the city, the country and now, after the pandemic, the world who loves Jesus and is called to the ministry of prayer.

As you read, see yourself there at the 4th Watch with us. I am teaching you by example how to declare. Once you get the hang of it, and you begin to feel the nudging of the Holy Ghost telling you to add more words to your declaration, use the space provided in the physical edition of this book to do it. If you don't have a physical edition, secure yourself a notebook to write your declarations down. And please, for all of you technology evangelists out there, don't depend solely on technology when you are writing your new laws. Smart phones are great until they aren't smart anymore. Data can be lost. Take pen to paper and write out your new laws. Then, if possible, back them up on a computer. Finally, when you get to the last chapter entitled Create, you will be asked to put into practice everything you have learned thus far. I will ask you to write your own personal declaration. Don't worry, once again, I have included a model for you. I have added to this book my own personal declaration.

THE REALM OF DECLARATORY GRACE

Use the parts that apply to you until you feel the Holy Spirit nudging you to create your own written law.

If you have any questions, or comments please reach out. if you want information on how to join with us virtually or in person for the 4th Watch please reach out. Email me at doingbusinesswithgod@gmail.com

Welcome to *The Realm of Declaratory Grace Workbook*. I cannot wait to see the amazing things you create. Change the world by doing business with God.

Sincerely,

Catrina J. Sparkman

Introduction

The Power & Purpose of Declaration

I am convinced that there is a realm in prayer that we enter where we no longer pray; we say. This is a concept that I have both personally pondered and spoken about for many years. I've taught it to my own intercessory prayer team and to intercessors across the world. I call it the realm of Declaratory Grace. In this realm, God the Creator takes off His signet ring and tells the one petitioning Him to write a new law. In this realm, you move from being a mere supplicant and you enter into partnership with God regarding the matter you have before Him in prayer. You have The Father's full attention and support. He doesn't tell you what to pray. He lets you decide.

You might be thinking right now to yourself as you read this, that this sounds beautiful in theory, but

THE REALM OF DECLARATORY GRACE

also very fanciful. To that I will say, there is biblical precedent for this in the book of Esther. Just in case you already know the story well, I'll just give you the highlights. The book of Esther tells the story of Haman, the enemy of the Jews, who legalized the total annihilation of the Jewish community living in the Persian empire. He had gone through all the proper channels to make certain their destruction was legalized and thus binding.

When Xerxes, the king, discovered that Haman's genocidal plot included Esther, his queen, he dealt swiftly with Haman. He ordered Haman and his sons to be hung on the gallows that Haman had constructed for Mordecai, Esther's uncle. The king also gave Esther all of Haman's property. While this was justice for Esther, the death warrant had already been signed against her family and her people. Esther fell on her knees before the king and begged him for the lives of her family members and her nation. She asked the king to reverse the destruction order that Haman had put into motion.

King Xerxes wanted to grant Esther's request, but it wasn't that simple. He explained to Esther the legality of the situation: the king's signet ring signed Haman's order, and according to Persian law, no decree signed into order with the king's signet ring can be reversed. He told her that what she could do, however, was to write a new law. King Xerxes gave his signet ring to Mordecai and told him and Esther to write a new decree. The king's secretaries were summoned, and as Mordecai dictated the new law, they wrote.

The day chosen for the Jew's destruction would have been in our calendar time, March 7th of the coming year. Mordecai writes his decree on June 25th. That meant they have less than one year to proclaim the new law that would thwart Haman's decree. Reader, please understand me when I tell you that King Xerxes empire was vast. There were no planes, trains, or automobiles, or electric powered boats. They had horses. Really fast horses, especially bred for the king's service. Scripture says that once the new law was written, swift messengers were deployed, and the message was carried to the Jews, the princes, the governors, and local officials of all the 127 provinces stretching from India to Ethiopia (Esther 8:9). Future more, the decree was written in the scripts and languages of all the peoples of the empire, including the Jews, so that everyone

THE REALM OF DECLARATORY GRACE

could understand.

According to the new law that Mordecai had written, every Jew in every city now had the legal authority to defend their lives. They had the right to kill, slaughter, and annihilate anyone of any nationality or province who might attack them, their children, or their wives. They also had the legal right to take the property of whatever enemies attempted to attack them (Esther 8:11).

Once the new law was written and dispatched to the people, it was declared. It was spoken in every tongue. It was declared to rulers and peasants alike. From the oldest to the youngest, everyone understood that on March 7th if an enemy came to attack you or your household, you had the right to get violent. Deadly violent. You have the legal right to take their lives and their property by force. We are in the book of Esther, but this is also Matthew 11:12 being lived out:

And from the days of John the Baptist until now, the kingdom of heaven suffers violence, and the violent take it by force (Matt 11:12 NKJV).

Everyone heard, understood and had to abide by

Mordecai's decree—be they thrones, rulers, principalities, or people. Reader, do you see where I am going with this?

For the purposes of this study, I want you to see your relationship with God, like Queen Esther's relationship with King Xerxes. Xerxes was her king and her husband. Like any wise woman, Esther had to learn how to navigate between the two roles. Let's not forget Esther got her job in the first place because the former queen, Vashti, couldn't successfully discern and navigate between the two roles. She didn't know when to deal with Xerxes as husband and when to approach him in his office as the Head of State. God is our Father and our King. We as believers must learn to navigate between when He is in his official capacity of Ruler of the Multiverse and when he is well... daddy.

Of course, He is always both, but if we don't understand how to approach Him, we, as believers, can be left feeling disappointed and confused. I've heard people say things like, "If God loves us, then why does cancer exist?" Or "Why do so many bad things happen to good people?" Oftentimes when I hear statements like this, I realize that the people speaking don't really

THE REALM OF DECLARATORY GRACE

understand government or God. There are two simple truths about God that will never change. Number one: God is perfectly just, and number two: He is on my side. One truth doesn't exist without the next.

Because our God is perfectly just, when the accuser of the brethren comes before him with a lawful petition against you, when the accuser stands before Him with evidence, the murder weapon, flowcharts, facts and figures; and, when there is no intercessor there to stand in the gap and object, the King of the Multiverse, who is also perfectly just, grants the adversary his request.

Well, dear reader, you may ask, how do I know God is on our side? I know because Psalm 8 tells me that out of the mouths of sucklings and babes God has ordained His praise to silence the foe and the avenger. That tells me that when I open my mouth, I can release a sound that shuts every attack aimed my way down. From both my enemies and my foes. Let me explain the difference. The word 'foe' refers to your sworn enemy. He hates you and me both, because we live and because we are of the Adamic race. He hates us because God has set his seal of love and approval upon us. The word 'avenger' refers to the adversary that has a legitimate right to come against you. This is usually because of sin, both personal sins, and bloodline curses). Psalm 8 tells me I can release a sound that can silence both my swore enemy and the one who has a legal claim against me.

Psalm 8 also tells me something else: the words that come out of my month can create a city of refuge that will protect me from the destroyer. Another way to say this, is to say that God is on my side.

I've named this book *The Realm of Declaratory Grace Workbook* because as you rise daily and anoint yourself with oil, you will do the work of reordering your world with your mouth. You will decree a new thing over your life and it will be established (Job 22:28) for you.

So, now that you understand your legal authority and your God given permission to do this, let me tell you why you must do it. There are some things that have been spoken over your life by people in authority that have become law for you. It could be parents, deceased relatives, supervisors, or church people. You could have even spoken death and destruction unknowingly

THE REALM OF DECLARATORY GRACE

with your own tongue. Those careless words are living and active in your life. Every day you say things out of habit like, "I'm so tired and fed up!" So, each day you wake up feeling unrested, with little or no tolerance. Your grandmother may have declared, one day in a fit of despair, 'No one in this family will ever amount to anything!' She's been dead for over twenty years, and no one in your entire family seems to be able to catch a break or get anywhere because those demonically inspired words are still living, active, working in the earth. Since no one else with authority has spoken up and said otherwise, that spoken word curse stands as law in the earth.

This book is God, The Uncontested King of Everything, offering you His signet ring. It's an invitation to declare some new promises over yourself, your family, and your nation as well — if you can catch the vision. This workbook is your invitation to write some new laws. I sense in my spirit that some of you are still not convinced. How does this work? Or better yet, why does it work? Let me explain.

We are made in the image and likeness of our Creator, God. We can create because He creates. Everything He made he spoke into existence. The only time God ever became 'hands on' during the creation process was when He made you and me. God Almighty stooped down. He took dust from the earth, divinity from Himself, formed it into a creation call mankind. I've watched people change the whole trajectory of their lives simply by declaring. I've watched a chronically homeless young man declare himself from homelessness into a job that paid his living expenses. I've watched a young woman working as a maid in a low budget motel declare herself into a fully funded master's degree program and then into her dream job as a social worker. So yes, it absolutely does work.

Another reason it works is something I like to call the 24/7s. That's short for Psalms 24: 7 and Proverbs 24:7. Psalms 24:7 says, *lift up your head o you Gates and be ye lifted up you everlasting doors and the King of Glory Shall come in. Who is the King of Glory, the Lord God, strong and Mighty.* I love this passage. I quote it often. And if you really want to understand who you are in relationship to our God, this verse should be repeated over and over again.

THE REALM OF DECLARATORY GRACE

Psalm 24: 7 tells us something very important about our spiritual identity. This verse tells us we are gates and doors, and that we are eternal. When we lift our heads in worship, in praise, in adoration to Him, when we look to the hills from where our help comes from, when we look up, The King of Glory will enter the Earth. Not as the Prince of Peace, or as the Lamb of God. No, this verse tells us that when we lift our bowed down head, God comes into the earth ready for battle.

He comes into the earth through our mouths. Through our worship and our declaration. I know the Lord uses the vehicle of our mouth to enter the Earth, because of the other 24/7. Proverbs 24:7 tells us this: *Wisdom is too high for a fool. He will not open his mouth at the gate.*

Psalm 24/7 gives us a directive. Proverbs 24/7 give us a warning. It's stupid to keep silent at the gate when the King of Glory is waiting to enter the earth realm through your mouth. The 24/7's positioning in scripture tells us how often we should heed them—24/7, all the time.

I hope I have given you enough evidence. I hope you

believe me enough to lift up your bowed down head and make some new laws at the gate.

DECLARATORY GRACE OILS

HOW TO USE THESE OILS

Anoint yourself daily with Live the first oil in the series and proclaim out loud the accompanying declaration for the next forty days or until you feel a release in your spirit telling you it is time to move to the next oil. When the declaration is true for you, it's time to move on. Experts tell us it takes anywhere between 21-54 days to build a habit. Prayerfully consider how many days you should use each oil. After you have spent the required amount of time anointing and speaking, move on to the next oil in the series: Stand.

Oils in the Declaratory Grace line

1. Live (unity)

2. Stand, (Union, Division, Witness)

3. Remember- (Resurrection, Divine completeness)

4. Thrive, (Creation)

5. Laughter (Grace, God's goodness)

6. Return (Weakness of man, Manifestation of sin)

7. Keep (Completion, Spiritual perfection)

8. Release (New beginnings)

9. Expect (Fruit of the Spirit)

10. Create (Testimony, Law and Responsibility)

1

THE OIL OF LIVE

(UNITY)

On the day you were born, your cord was not cut, nor were you washed with water to make you clean, nor were you rubbed with salt or wrapped in cloths. [5] No one looked on you with pity or had compassion enough to do any of these things for you. Rather, you were thrown out into the open field, for on the day you were born you were despised. [6] "'Then I passed by and saw you kicking about in your blood, and as you lay there in your blood I said to you, "Live!"[7] I made you grow like a plant of the field. You grew and developed and entered puberty. Your breasts had formed and your hair had grown, yet you were stark naked. [8] "'Later I passed by, and when I looked at you and saw that you were old enough for love, I spread the corner of my garment over you and covered your naked body. I gave you my solemn oath and entered into a covenant with you, declares the Sovereign Lord, and you became mine.

Ezekiel 16;4-8 Niv

The Oil of Live

Live Oil includes a blend of cardamom, lavender in an olive oil base. Cardamom essential oil is known for its ability to improve concentration, fortify mental functioning. It is considered a calming tonic for the mind and emotions. Cardamom soothes nervous tension, brings ease to an upset stomach and the digestive system. The scent of cardamom is effective in relieving nausea and vomiting associated with pregnancy and chemotherapy. The scent is grounding and revives the appetite for life. Lavender essential oil promotes relaxation, is affective against anxiety, insomnia, depression, fungal infections, menstrual cramps, promotes respiratory health, and is a natural bug repellent.

Who Should Use This Oil:

The Oil of Live is for those suffering from a life-threatening illness, and all forms of dis-ease, (physical, mental, or emotional). Live is for the brokenhearted, the abandoned, the suicidal, and the one barely holding on to life. Live is also for anyone not living their best life.

When to Use this Oil:

You should anoint yourself with Live when your future is threatened with abortion. Anoint yourself with Live. Bind yourself to life and come into unity (agreement) with the future that God, your Father and Creator, always intended for you.

A Message from the Father about Life:

I know that life has not always been good. I know that life has not always been kind. I know that life has not always proven fair. On top of all of that, it appears that I, the Lord, Am the one who has forsaken you and orchestrated all of your woes. This is not true, and yet even right now as I speak, I know that life and people have disappointed you so many times and although you want to believe it.... it is impossible for you to do so right now. But know this, Beloved, I cannot lie. I AM not like a man or a woman in that I change My mind. My thoughts towards you are always gracious. Trust Me when I say it will get better than this. Each day hereafter will be better than this. Anoint yourself with life. Make a conscious choice to live today. It will get better than this. Pour a small amount of oil into your hands, rub it in, cup your hands over your nose and mouth and inhale deeply. Now live. You are Mine and I never abandon My own. I will tell you this again, one day very soon, and on that day, you will be able to believe it.

Declaration for the Oil of Live:

Your declaration is simple:

Today, I choose to live and not die. I bind myself to life, and when I say life, I mean God's abundant pressed down, shaken together, running over, overflowing into every cell of my being kind of life, and then into every cell of everyone I encounter kind of life. In fact, I am going to be so full of life that I will be like Jesus in the crowd of people and the prophet in

THE REALM OF DECLARATORY GRACE

2 King 13:21, who was buried in his tomb. All anyone in need of healing will have to do is brush up against my clothes or touch my bones and they will also have life. Not only will I be healed, I will be a healer. I will see the goodness of the Lord in the Land of the Living. What God has waiting for me is better than this. I decree and I declare that life more abundantly is headed my way, and it is way better than this.

When you are ready to write some new laws, in the space provided on the next page write your own decree.

MY PERSONAL DECREE TO LIVE

2

THE OIL OF STAND

(Union, Division, Witness)

*Children, obey your parents in the Lord, for this is right.
² "Honor your father and mother"—which is the first
commandment with a promise — ³ "so that it may go
well with you and that you may enjoy long life on the
earth." ⁴ Fathers, do not exasperate your children; instead, bring them up in the training and instruction of
the Lord. ⁵ Slaves, obey your earthly masters with respect
and fear, and with sincerity of heart, just as you would
obey Christ. ⁶ Obey them not only to win their favor
when their eye is on you, but as slaves of Christ, doing
the will of God from your heart. ⁷ Serve wholeheartedly,
as if you were serving the Lord, not people, ⁸ because you
know that the Lord will reward each one for whatever*

good they do, whether they are slave or free. [9] *And masters, treat your slaves in the same way. Do not threaten them, since you know that he who is both their Master and yours is in heaven, and there is no favoritism with him.* [10] *Finally, be strong in the Lord and in his mighty power.* [11] *Put on the full armor of God, so that you can take your stand against the devil's schemes.* [12] *For our struggle is not against flesh and blood, but against the rulers, against the authorities, against the powers of this dark world and against the spiritual forces of evil in the heavenly realms.* [13] *Therefore, put on the full armor of God, so that when the day of evil comes, you may be able to stand your ground, and after you have done everything, to stand.* [14] *Stand firm then, with the belt of truth buckled around your waist, with the breastplate of righteousness in place,* [15] *and with your feet fitted with the readiness that comes from the gospel of peace.* [16] *In addition to all this, take up the shield of faith, with which you can extinguish all the flaming arrows of the evil one.* [17] *Take the helmet of salvation and the sword of the Spirit, which is the word of God.* [18] *And pray in the Spirit on all occasions with all kinds of prayers and requests. With this in mind, be alert and always keep on praying for all the Lord's people.*

THE REALM OF DECLARATORY GRACE

Ephesians 6

The Oil of Stand

The Oil of Stand contains a harmonious blend of Cedar, Frankincense, Ylang-Ylang in an Olive oil bases. Three powerful inflammation fighting essential oils. Cedarwood diminishes stress and anxiety and fights muscle spasms and headaches. It is also useful in the treatment of dandruff, alopecia, and hair thinning. Frankincense fights against joint pain and inflammation of the gut. Frankincense essential oil is also believed to be effective in fighting breast, prostate, pancreatic, skin, and colon cancer cells, preventing the spread of certain cancer cells, and reducing the side effects of treatment. Ylang- Ylang essential oil is also anti-inflammatory. This oil also has a calming effect, decreasing blood pressure and heart rate and stops anxiety in its tracks.

Who Should Use The Oil Of Stand:

Fathers and mothers, small children, adult children,

pre-teens, teenagers, employers and employees, landlords and renters, brothers, and sisters, those engaging in commerce—whether they be buyers or sellers, teachers and students, those who love God and desire to walk upright. Most people start talking about this passage in Ephesians at verse 10—the full armor of God. However, the majority of this passage is about how we, as believers, should relate to each other. How we should interact with our children. How we should view our parents. How bosses and employees should relate to one another. (all people we view as having power over us at some point.) Once we come into proper relationship with the people in our world, then we are told to put on the full armor of God. God is so serious about us being in right relationship with people that he tells us in Matt 5:23-24, If you are praying and remember that your brother has an ought against you, stop praying, get up and go be reconciled with your brother and then come back and see me later. If this is God's response to us when we seek to spend time in worship and prayer with Him, how much more when we prepare for battle? I tell you the truth, the spiritual armor of God will not help any of us if we are not properly aligned with the correct people in the earth.

THE REALM OF DECLARATORY GRACE

When To Use This Oil:

Anoint yourself with the Oil of Stand when you are out of alignment with people or with God. Use the Oil of Stand when you need God to strengthen your back. Use the Oil of Stand when you need to deal with people in a way that is fitting and honoring to God. Also use the Oil of Stand when you need to wage war against the evil one.

A Message From The Father About Standing:

Dear One,

Know that I always put first things first. This is why the first ten verses of Ephesians 6 tells you how to treat people. The last eight verses tell you how to do battle with and overcome the evil one. You cannot have the latter before the former, and the same armor that you need to adorn yourself with to fight your unseen enemy is the same armor you need to put on so that you can deal correctly and justly with your fellow man. I AM relational. I expect My people to be so as well. Heaven cares how you conduct business.

I care about your relationships. You stand firm when these relationships are right to the best of your ability. When you are in right standing in the seen world, you can conquer your foes in the unseen world.

Declaration for the Oil of Stand

Dear Lord, today I make the choice to stand firm in you. Help me love my mother, my brother, and my sister. Help me love my enemies. Help me love my boss and my neighbor. Help me, love (fill in the name of people you need to put here). Today, I declare that my back is strong. I am fit for the task that God has called me to. Fighting the devil is easy. Loving people is hard. Today I will live, stand and love in a way that both honors and pleases my King and brings honor and acclaim to His unconquerable name.

After you have recited the above decree for a while, you may be led to personalize your declaration to stand. Do so in the space provided on the next page.

MY PERSONAL DECREE TO STAND

3

THE OIL OF REMEMBER

(Resurrection, Divine Completeness)

My dear brothers and sisters, take note of this: Everyone should be quick to listen, slow to speak and slow to become angry, because human anger does not produce the righteousness that God desires. Therefore, get rid of all moral filth and the evil that is so prevalent and humbly accept the word planted in you which can save you. Do not merely listen to the word and so deceive yourselves. Do what it says. Anyone who listens to the word but does not do what it says is like someone who looks at his face in a mirror, and after looking at himself, goes away and immediately forgets what he looks like. But whoever looks intently into the perfect law that gives freedom and continues in it—not forgetting what they have heard but doing it—they will be blessed in what they do. Those that consider themselves religious and yet do not keep a tight rein on their tongues deceive themselves, and their religion is worthless. Religion that God our Father accepts as pure and faultless is this: to look after orphans and widows in their distress and to keep oneself from being polluted by the world.

James 1: 19-27

The Oil of Remember

The Oil of Remember contains a blend of Spearmint, Rosemary, Cinnamon, Clove, and Anise essential oil in an Olive oil base. Spearmint essential oil is believed to relieve headaches and stress, boost digestion, and increase focus. Rosemary Essential oil improves brain function and strengthens memory. Clove essential oil is anticandidal and antifungal. It boosts the immune system and increases blood circulation. Anise aids in pain relief, promotes immune system health, and is often used in the treatment of respiratory disorders. Cinnamon essential oil in concert with the other oils in this blend is believed to help the body defend itself against heart disease, high cholesterol and neurological health disorders like Alzheimer's and Parkinson's disease.

Who Should Use the Oil of Remember:

Anyone suffering from memory loss or cognitive decline who is believing God for a turnaround should use the oil of remember. Anyone who needs to make their calling and election in Christ sure should use the Oil of Remember. Anyone who needs to put a tight rein on their tongue should use the Oil of Remember.

When to Use this Oil:

When you need to remind yourself, your situation and the powers of hell that God keeps His promises, anoint yourself with the Oil of Remember.

A Message from the Father About Remember:

Dear One,

THE REALM OF DECLARATORY GRACE

When you remember, you are making a conscious choice to re-enlist. To become a member again. Narrow is the road that leads to salvation. Broad is the road that leads to destruction. There are many ways to die, but only one way to live. Jesus told you what that way was during His time on earth. He said, 'man shall not live by bread alone but by every word that proceeds out of the mouth of God.' My Word, My Son, the Second part of the triune God, Who became flesh, is life. You have Christians all day looking at the Word of God, consuming the Word, but when it comes to informing their decisions, applying it to their everyday lives, they forget. When you use the oil of remembrance, you are making a conscious choice not to forget. You say, today, I shall remember my Father and His Word. I will keep a tight rein over my tongue. I will do everything in my power (which is really His power) to protect the poor, the orphaned, and the needy. I will live out His Word today in practice, thought, speech, and deed. When you use the oil of remembrance, you are saying, 'I re-enlist as a soldier in the kingdom of God today. I de-enlist as a citizen of the world—it's culture, values and norms.' This is what you do when you remember.

Declaration for the Oil of Remember:

Today, I choose to remember God's law. I rid myself of all the moral filth in my life that is so prevalent in my world, whether it be gossip, slander or pornography, human anger (fill in the blank of whatever you need). I humbly accept Your Word, Lord. It has been planted inside of me to save me. The soil of my heart and the soil of my mind is good. I believe Isaiah 55:11. The word written inside the Holy Bible came out of the mouth of the Most High God. His Word cannot return to Him void. It will accomplish what he sent it forth to do. It will prosper in the thing He has sent His Word into. I am the thing that God has sent His Word into this morning. God's Word is prospering inside of me.

When you are ready to do so, in the space provided on the next page, write your personalized decree to remember.

THE REALM OF DECLARATORY GRACE

MY PERSONAL DECREE TO REMEMBER

4

THE OIL OF THRIVE

(CREATION)

I will bless the Lord at all times; His praise shall continually be in my mouth. ² My soul shall make its boast in the Lord; The humble shall hear of it and be glad. ³ Oh, magnify the Lord with me, And let us exalt His name together. ⁴ I sought the Lord, and He heard me, And delivered me from all my fears. ⁵ They looked to Him and were radiant, And their faces were not ashamed. ⁶ This poor man cried out, and the Lord heard him, And saved him out of all his troubles. ⁷ The angel of the Lord encamps all around those who fear Him, And delivers them. ⁸ Oh, taste and see that the Lord is good; Blessed is the man who trusts in Him! ⁹ Oh, fear the Lord, you His saints! There is no want to those who fear Him. ¹⁰ The young lions lack and suffer hunger; But those who seek the Lord shall not lack any good thing. ¹¹ Come, you *children, listen to me; I will teach you the fear of the Lord. ^{12} Who is the man who desires life? And loves many days, that he may see good? ^{13} Keep your tongue from evil, And your lips from speaking deceit. ^{14} Depart from evil and do good; Seek peace and pursue it. ^{15} The eyes of the Lord are on the righteous, And His ears are open to their cry. ^{16} The face of the Lord is against those who do evil, To cut off the remembrance of them from the earth. ^{17} The righteous cry out, and the Lord hears, And delivers them out of all their troubles. ^{18} The Lord is near to those who have a broken heart, And saves such as have a contrite spirit. ^{19} Many are the afflictions of the righteous, But the Lord delivers him out of them all. ^{20} He guards all his bones; Not one of them is broken. ^{21} Evil shall slay the wicked, And those who hate the righteous shall be condemned. ^{22} The Lord redeems the soul of His servants, And none of those who trust in Him shall be condemned.*

Psalm 34

The Oil of Thrive

The oil of Thrive is composed of Geranium, Ylang-Ylang, Clary Sage and Lavender essential oils in an

Olive Oil base. Geranium essential oil is known for its antimicrobial, antifungal and antiviral properties. It is used as an aid against anxiety, depression and skin infections, as well as pain management. Ylang-Ylang essential oil is anti-inflammatory. This essential oil is known for its ability to produce a calming effect upon the body. Ylang-Ylang essential oil is also used to decrease blood pressure and heart rate and to stop anxiety and panic attacks. Clary Sage essential oil is a natural anti-depressant, used in the alleviation of menopause symptoms and reducing menstrual cramps. Lavender essential oil promotes relaxation, treats anxiety, fungal infections, allergies, depression, insomnia, eczema, nausea and menstrual cramps. The essential oils in this blend work together in harmony to help the user thrive.

A Message from the Father about Thrive:

Dear One,

To thrive means to replenish, to flourish, to produce.

When you are in survival mode, all you can do is hold on. Wait for your salvation to come. Wait for deliverance to come. In Survival mode, hair doesn't grow. Your body won't release excess weight. It holds on to everything—even things it doesn't need, things that won't serve it anymore (like waste and pain.) The body holds on to these useless things because it doesn't know when it will be hungry again, when it will need to feed. You can't create anything new in survival mode. In survival mode, your only job to hold on. In survival, you store everything in the rainy-day fund. The only problem with that is that every day it rains. Every single day is cloudy with no chance of sun. As a result, you are flooded with disappointment and regret. And yet, even still, somewhere in the back of your mind you can hear the still small voice of the Father telling you to hold on. Where survival mode represents famine, thrive represents feast. So come My love, taste and see that the Lord is good. I had Noah build an ark for survival. But after My wrath had ended, and the waters receded, the command he heard was to come out of the boat, to replenish and thrive. Replenish the earth and thrive. Prosper, bloom, succeed, and grow well. Then there was David. David recited the 34th psalm at his lowest point. He had been

THE REALM OF DECLARATORY GRACE

driven away from his homeland by his father-in-law, a homicidal, rejected, deposed king. David was forced to seek refuge and protection for his family from his enemies. What was David's crime? Only that he dared to believe and walk in the promises of God. That by itself, My love, is enough for your enemies to wage war against you. For them to come and eviscerate your land. That you would dare to believe the whispers of the Shepard King over the wicked stepfather. I spoke to David when he was just a ruddy boy watching over the sheep, the least in his house, the least in his father's eyes. I spoke to him as a boy and told him I would make him King. That I would give him a dynasty that would never end. That little boy who worshiped Me in the wilderness dared to believe Me, and, as you see, I kept My Word. Jesus is from the line of David. And His kingdom will never end. David's response when he was backed against a wall, forced to pretend a moment of madness before his enemy was to come to himself, to remember My word and to replenish himself by drinking of Me. Now I invite you to do the same thing. Oh, taste and see, beloved that the Lord is good.

Who Should Use this Oil:

Anyone who is ready to walk into the next level of freedom should use the Oil of Thrive. Anyone who is tired of merely existing and surviving should anoint themselves by faith and move into the land of thrive. Anyone who is called to create something new, something the world has never seen before should anoint themselves with the Oil of Thrive.

When to use the Oil of Thrive:

Use the Oil of Thrive when you hear God whispering to your heart, beckoning you that the storm is over and that it is time to come out of the boat. The King of Kings, the Great I AM, is holding out His hand to you. Anoint yourself with the oil of Thrive. Recite the 34th Psalm. As you do, see yourself in your mind's eye, climbing out of your boat. Use the oil of Thrive when you feel like you've failed. Like the promises of God will never come to pass. When decimation is all around you but you see just a tiny sliver of light.

THE REALM OF DECLARATORY GRACE

Declaration for the Oil of Thrive

Dearest Father, Lord Jesus, and Almighty Holy Ghost, today I accept the totality of your deliverance plan for my life as I get out of the boat. I admit I have been in survival mode for so long that I don't even fully understand what it means to thrive. But I trust you and I lean and depend on you. Today, I will make it my business to eat and drink deeply of you. Like David, I refresh myself in your presence. Like Noah, I say goodbye to my ark of safety. I step out into a new world. Today I thrive.

When you are ready to do so, in the space provided on the next page, write your personalized decree to thrive.

MY PERSONAL DECREE TO THRIVE

5

THE OIL OF LAUGHTER

(GRACE, GOD'S GOODNESS)

Now the Lord was gracious to Sarah as he had said, and the Lord did for Sarah what he had promised. ² Sarah became pregnant and bore a son to Abraham in his old age, at the very time God had promised him. ³ Abraham gave the name Isaac[a] to the son Sarah bore him. ⁴ When his son Isaac was eight days old, Abraham circumcised him, as God commanded him. ⁵ Abraham was a hundred years old when his son Isaac was born to him.⁶ Sarah said, "God has brought me laughter, and everyone who hears about this will laugh with me." ⁷ And she added, "Who would have said to Abraham that Sarah would nurse children? Yet I have borne him a son in his old age."

Genesis 21: 1-7

A cheerful heart is good medicine, but a crushed spirit dries up the bones.

Proverbs 17:2

The Oil of Laughter:

The oil of Laughter is comprised of Ylang-Ylang, Clary Sage, Ginger and Lemongrass essential oils in an Olive oil base. Ylang- Ylang essential oil is anti-inflammatory. This essential oil is known for its ability to produce a calming effect. Ylang-Ylang essential oil is also used to decrease blood pressure and heart rate and to stop anxiety and panic attacks. Clary Sage essential oil is a natural anti-depressant, is used in the alleviation of menopause symptoms and reducing menstrual cramps. Ginger essential oil includes over 40 antioxidant properties. This essential oil protects the skin against free radicals, improves elasticity and rejuvenates the complexion, and safeguards the skin from premature ageing. Lemongrass is used for pain relief, blood sugar regulation, improved digestion, and stress and anxiety relief.

THE REALM OF DECLARATORY GRACE

A Message From The Father About Laughter:

Dear One,

Sarah laughed at the promises of God when I came and told her that she would bear a son in her old age, in a barren body that had already failed her many times in her youth. The moment the Word of the Lord came to her, she should have laughed at life, and at the enemy that had robbed her of the very thing she was created to do. Nobody likes to be laughed at. And to laugh at a god is an act of war. I asked Sarah, 'why did she laugh?' not because I wanted to stop her laughter. My aim was to redirect her warfare. Eventually, she got the point. By Genesis 21:6, I had redirected her laughter. Naomi laughed too. When she returned home to Israel from the land of Moab broken, and alone with no covering except that of her also widowed daughter-in-law, Ruth, she said, 'Call me Mara because I am bitter. I went away full, but the Lord has brought me back empty.' She said that the Almighty One had brought misfortune upon her. Indeed, a formidable foe had brought misfortune upon her, but the enemy that pillaged and destroyed her family—killed her husband

and her sons, was not the Almighty One. Like Sarah, Naomi was mis-informed. Her warfare needed to be redirected, too. Just as I raised up Isaac for Sarah and Obed for Naomi and Ruth, I can also do what seems to be impossible for you. Choose instead to believe Me, then Anoint yourself with the oil of laughter this morning and re-direct your laugh. Nobody likes to be mocked, to be laughed at. But to laugh at a god is an act of war. Laugh at the devil who thinks he has you on the ropes, laugh at the one who thinks he has you down on the floor, never to arise again before the final count. Throw your head back and laugh hard. Laugh until tears roll down your face. Laugh, and as you laugh, I will come and stand behind you and the enemy will see that the power you are working with now is not your own. He will buckle and he will bow at your laugh.

Who Should Use the Oil of Laughter:

Anyone who is experiencing sickness in the physical body should use the Oil of Laughter. Anyone who is tormented by the spirit of depression, and or heaviness of heart should use the Oil of Laughter. Anyone who has experienced heartbreak or grief should anoint themselves with Laughter. Anyone waiting on a ridiculous promise from God should anoint themselves by faith with Laughter.

When To Use the Oil of Laughter:

When trouble comes to your home, laugh. When the evil one comes to remind you of what God has not done, what promises have not yet been fulfilled, anoint yourself with the oil of laughter and laugh. When you want to celebrate, laugh. When you want to torment the one who has been tormenting you, anoint yourself with laughter and laugh. When you need to remind the evil one that no weapon formed against you will prosper and every tongue that rises against you: you shall condemn, anoint yourself with the Oil of Laughter and laugh.

Declaration for the Oil Of Laughter:

Dearest Father, Sweet Jesus and Precious Holy Spirit, I thank you right now for a spirit of laughter. I thank you for your Word in Proverbs 17:22 that proclaims that a merry heart is good medicine. I declare that not only is my laughter routing the enemy that seeks to make war against me and my loved ones right now, as I laugh, my spirit is being mended. Strength and vitality is coming into my bones. My organs muscles, and connective tissues are being restored. My brain is being rebooted. My brain is being rebooted. (Say that as many times as you need to.) Laughter is even healing my soul. And to every spiritual weapon formed and fashioned against me and those I love, I cast you down and condemn you to death. (Insert laughter here) Shame be upon you for underestimating the Almighty One's great love for me. You thought you had me, devil. You thought my story was over. You thought my name was defeated. From this day forward, I am no longer the one you laid waste to and destroyed. All of heaven shall know that His Grace is upon me. Heaven calls me the Comeback Kid.

When you are ready to do so, in the space provided n the next page, write your personalized decree to laugh.

THE REALM OF DECLARATORY GRACE

MY PERSONAL DECREE TO LAUGH

6

THE OIL OF RETURN

(Weakness of Man, Manifestation of Sin)

[11] Jesus continued: "There was a man who had two sons. [12] The younger one said to his father, 'Father, give me my share of the estate.' So he divided his property between them. [13] "Not long after that, the younger son got together all he had, set off for a distant country and there squandered his wealth in wild living. [14] After he had spent everything, there was a severe famine in that whole country, and he began to be in need. [15] So he went and hired himself out to a citizen of that country, who sent him to his fields to feed pigs. [16] He longed to fill his stomach with the pods that the pigs were eating, but no one gave him anything. [17] "When he came to his senses, he said, 'How many of my father's hired servants have food to spare, and here I am starving to death! [18] I will

set out and go back to my father and say to him: Father, I have sinned against heaven and against you. [19] I am no longer worthy to be called your son; make me like one of your hired servants.' [20] So he got up and went to his father. "But while he was still a long way off, his father saw him and was filled with compassion for him; he ran to his son, threw his arms around him and kissed him. [21] "The son said to him, 'Father, I have sinned against heaven and against you. I am no longer worthy to be called your son.' [22] "But the father said to his servants, 'Quick! Bring the best robe and put it on him. Put a ring on his finger and sandals on his feet. [23] Bring the fattened calf and kill it. Let's have a feast and celebrate. [24] For this son of mine was dead and is alive again; he was lost and is found.' So they began to celebrate. [25] "Meanwhile, the older son was in the field. When he came near the house, he heard music and dancing. [26] So he called one of the servants and asked him what was going on. [27] 'Your brother has come,' he replied, 'and your father has killed the fattened calf because he has him back safe and sound.' [28] "The older brother became angry and refused to go in. So his father went out and pleaded with him. [29] But he answered his father, 'Look! All these years I've been slaving for you and never disobeyed your orders. Yet you never gave me even a young goat so I could celebrate with my friends. ³⁰ But when this son of yours who has squandered your property with prostitutes comes home, you kill the fattened calf for him!' ³¹ "'My son,' the father said, 'you are always with me, and everything I have is yours. ³² But we had to celebrate and be glad, because this brother of yours was dead and is alive again; he was lost and is found.'"

Luke 15

The Oil of Return:

The Oil of Return is comprised of Hyssop, Cedarwood, Calamus Root, Thyme, Patchouli, Clove, and Ginger essential oils in an olive oil blend. Hyssop essential oil is used to fight infection, purify the body, and to alleviate asthma and other respiratory symptoms. Clove essential oil has an anticandidal and antifungal effect, which boosts the immune system and increases blood circulation. Calamus Root is used in the treatment of stomach problems, earaches, and skin problems, relieving inflammation, and headaches. This essential oil has also been used for hormone regulation to balance mood, sex drive, menstrual regularity and energy production and to treat psychological disorders such as depression. Calamus Root has also been used to treat disorders of the nervous system such as epilepsy and Parkinson's disease. Thyme essential oil is believed to normalize blood pressure, and reduces stress on the heart. This essential oil is also used to treat chest infection and cough. Thyme essential oil increases blood circulation, boosts the immune system, and aids in the detoxification of the body. Patchouli essential oil is used in the treatment of skin conditions, controlling appetite, and relieving depression. This oil is known for its ability to provide feelings of relaxation and ease stress or anxiety. Patchouli essential oil is also used for weight loss, pain relief, and to facilitate the healing of wounds. Cedarwood essential oil combats stress and anxiety, is useful in the treatment of dandruff, alopecia, and hair thinning, muscle spasms, and headaches. Ginger essential oil protects the skin against free radicals, improves elasticity and rejuvenates the complexion, and safeguards the skin from premature ageing.

A Message From The Father About Re-

THE REALM OF DECLARATORY GRACE

turning:

Dear One,

The word Re-turn means to turn again, to turn away. A righteous man falls seven times, but he gets back up. If he fell into sin seven times, what makes him righteous then, you might ask? He's got the understanding that I want all my children to have: Their rightness is not based on who they are or what they have done but completely and solely on who I AM and who they are to Me. The son of a king remains the son of a king whether he lives in the palace with the king, or chooses to wallow among whores in a brothel or with pigs in a slop house. Where he chooses to lay his head, what he chooses to do with his body, does not dictate his identity. It may dictate how he feels about his identity. But not one time while the son was laying down in the squalor did he cease to be the son of the king. And, most importantly, My love, at any moment he can re-turn to his Father.

When to Use this Oil:

Return is a great oil to anoint yourself with if you are

coming out of addiction, walking away from sin and breaking destructive cycles. If you have to re-turn 20 times a day, do it. Anoint yourself and turn again to the One who loves you, unconditionally and always.

Who Should Use The Oil Of Return:

The oil of Return is also good for people who need to return to a place of health and wellness, those showing signs of memory loss, those suffering from brain fog confusion, those dealing with mental disorders, compulsions, and those who find themselves in cyclical patterns.

Declaration For The Oil Of Return:

Dear Father God, Big Brother Jesus and Holy Spirit: I repent right now for any thoughts and deeds I have done that have not pleased You. I repent for every idol I have placed above You. Please break the stench of sin and death off my life, for you see, it follows me everywhere I go. I thank you for the example of the righteous man in scripture, who falls seven times and yet you welcome him with open arms because he has the understanding to get back up and turn again to

THE REALM OF DECLARATORY GRACE

You. Today I am that man. I re-turn again to You. I look to You, the Author and Finisher of my faith, to save and deliver me as only You can do. And when I come forth, and I will come forth, I will be made whole.

When you are ready to do so, in the space provided on the next page, write your personalized decree to return.

MY PERSONAL DECREE TO RETURN

7

THE OIL OF KEEP

(COMPLETION, SPIRITUAL PERFECTION)

"'The Lord bless you and keep you; [25] the Lord make his face shine on you and be gracious to you; [26] the Lord turn his face toward you and give you peace."

Numbers 6: 24-26

The Oil OF Keep:

The Oil of Keep is comprised of Peppermint essential oil, Eucalyptus essential oil, and Myrrh essential oil in an Olive oil base. Peppermint essential oil is known to reduce pain, headaches, and muscle fatigue. Peppermint essential oil is also used to improve clarity and mental functioning, and reduces stress. Eucalyptus essential oil protects the lungs, blocks asthma symptoms, relieves coughs, clears out the chest. Eucalyptus essential oil also eases join pain, controls blood sugar and is a natural bug repellant. Myrrh essential oil is a calming, meditative fragrance, with anti-cancer qualities. This powerful essential oil kills harmful bacteria, supports mouth health, and is used to clean and treat wounds.

A Message From The Father About Keeping:

Dear One,

To keep means to guard to preserve. I AM the Lord your God and I do not change. I've set keepers in every house and in every family line. I AM not like a man that I would lie, falter, waver, or change My mind. Keepers were a good idea when I established them in the bloodlines from the beginning, and they are a good idea now. I would that My people never return to slavery, so I set them in every house. In churches, you know them as prophets, and, when functioning correctly, they have the supernatural ability to preserve the flock and the house. In families, you know them as kinsmen redeemers/ blood avengers. Jesus is the firstborn of your kind. He is your Kinsmen Redeemer. With His blood sacrifice, He made you My kin. After He died, He descended into hell and took back everything stolen from humanity. When He took captivity captive (Ephesians 4:8) on your behalf, he became your avenger as well. The job of the keeper, the kinsman redeemer, is to buy the one being redeemed out of slavery and hold their freedom, their property, their resources in trust, until they can manage and hold on to it for themselves. The job of the blood avenger is to go to war against every enemy that would come against your family, your nation, your community. I have endowed you little one with the power to do this, but know this: redemption is always costly. Anoint yourself with the Oil of Keep when you are ready to pay the cost.

Who Should Use the Oil of Keep:

Parents, grandparents, teachers, pastors, prophets, Anyone who is called by God to do a work. Anyone who is called to safeguard or manage something should anoint themselves by faith with the Oil of

Keep. Anyone who has made a vow to the Lord.

When to Use This Oil:

Anoint yourself with the Oil of Keep when you are ready to stand in your family, your bloodline, your church, your community as the kinsman redeemer/blood avenger. Also anoint yourself with the Oil of Keep when you make a vow to the Lord, such as a vow of holiness, sexual purity, or a Nazarite vow. Anoint yourself with the Oil of Keep when you need to hold onto the promises of God with expectation. Also anoint yourself with the oil of keep when you stand as a watchman on the wall for your city, for your nation, for your church.

Declaration For the Oil of Keep:

I am anointed today to keep. I am anointed to hold on to the promises of God, and the people of God. I don't care what it looks like right now. I don't care what it sounds like right now. I don't even care what

THE REALM OF DECLARATORY GRACE

it feels like right now. I am anointed to hold on to the vision of peace, prosperity, and salvation that God has given me for my family, my posterity, my community and my nation. I am anointed to keep. That will never change. God has called me and set me on the wall of my family to be a Kinsmen Redeemer. So as a keeper, as a kinsmen redeemer for my family, I declare today, that as for me and my house we will serve God the Father, God the Son and God the Holy Spirit. I break any and every previously made family pacts made with death, darkness and destruction. I cast down every spoken word curse and every time released curse. As for me, as for my house, we will serve the one true King forever. We are forever in His hand, and no demon in hell can ever pluck my bloodline out.

When you are ready to do so, in the space provided on the next page, write your personalized decree to keep.

MY PERSONAL DECREE TO KEEP

8

THE OIL OF RELEASE

(New Beginnings)

But it is written, what no eye has seen, nor ear heard, Nor the human heart conceived. What God has prepared for those who love him.

1 Corinthians 2:9

The Oil of Release

The Oil of Release is a combination of Vetiver, Lavender, Clary Sage, Patchouli, Frankincense, and Geranium in an olive oil blend. All oils designed to fight anxiety and strengthen the heart. Vetiver essential oil is used to relieve stress, emotional traumas and shock, nervousness, insomnia, and joint and muscle pain, stings and burns. Lavender promotes relaxation, treats anxiety, fungal infections, allergies, depression, insomnia, eczema, nausea and menstrual cramps. Clary Sage essential oil is a natural anti-depressant, is used in the alleviation of menopause symptoms and reducing menstrual cramps. Patchouli essential oil is used in the treatment of skin conditions, controlling appetite, and relieving depression. This oil is known for its ability to provide feelings of relaxation and ease stress or anxiety. Patchouli essential oil is also used for weight loss, pain relief, and to facilitate the healing of wounds. Frankincense fights against joint pain and inflammation of the gut. Frankincense essential oil is also believed to be effective in fighting breast, prostate, pancreatic, skin, and colon cancer cells, preventing the spread of certain cancer cells, and reducing the side effects of treatment.

A Message From the Father About Release

The most important thing to remember about release

is that when God asks you to do it, it is not the same as taking a loss. Even when the moment feels like loss. When it feels like failure; when it feels like you are giving up or punking-out. My prompting to release is always an invitation into greatness. So go ahead Dear Heart, open your hand and release the thing that I AM is calling you to. What I have for you is so much better than the measly scraps of reality you now hold in your hand. I've dreamed of giving you this gift for a very long time. No eyes have ever seen this. No ears have ever heard it. The human mind can't even begin to conceive or dream of the great land your Father wishes to bestow upon you. The Evil One can, though, and this is why the spirit of anxiety causes your heart to race whenever you sense Me, prompting you to forgive or to release. Open your hand and tell the devil this: You can take these measly scraps, devil. My Father is the uncontested King of kings, and what He has for me is so much better than this.

Who Should Use The Oil of Release:

Anyone who needs to let go of something that is

holding them back should anoint themselves by faith with the Oil of Release. Anyone who needs to forgive themselves and others should anoint themselves by faith with the Oil of Release. Anyone who needs to release their voice should anoint themselves with the Oil of Release. Anyone who suffers from hording, or the spirit of lack needs to anoint themselves by faith with Release. Anyone who has trouble trusting God or who is plagued by a spirit of doubt should anoint themselves with Release.

When to Use this Oil:

There are many things we are called to release in this life. Sometimes God is calling for the release of your voice. Sometimes God is calling us to release old wounds, pain, grief, death, or useless paradigms and old mindsets. Sometimes God is calling for us to release people from past grievances or mistakes. As teachers and ministers of the Gospel, sometimes we are called to release those we have been given stewardship of. This becomes especially difficult when we believe those people are not ready to be released or that they are moving outside of God's divine plan or timing. As parents, we will all be called to release our children whether it's to the first day of kindergarten, off to college, and for those wayward children who refuse to receive instruction, for a season, you may be called to release them into the hands of the Almighty God. But here's the thing: no matter what God is calling us to release, release is always hard. Anoint yourself with the oil of release by adding a small drop to the palm of clean hands. Rub it in and cup your hands over your mouth and nose to fully take in the scent. As you do, picture in your mind the person, place, or thing in your hand that God is calling you to release.

Declaration For The Oil Of Release:

Dear Father God, Precious Holy Ghost, Savior Jesus, I sense in my Spirit today that you are inviting me into greatness and that the cost of admission into the greatness you have prepared for me is release. So today I accept your invitation into greatness. I open my hand. I open my mind, my spirit and my heart to you and I release.

When you are ready to do so, in the space provided on the next page, write your personalized decree to release.

MY PERSONAL DECREE TO RELEASE

9

THE OIL OF EXPECT

(FRUIT OF THE SPIRIT)

Now faith is the substance of things hoped for, the evidence of things not seen.

Hebrews 11:1

The Oil of Expectation:

The Oil of Expectation is a careful blend of Lavender, Ylang-Ylang, Lemongrass, Frankincense, Orange, Myrrh, and Peppermint essential oils in an Olive oil base. Lavender promotes relaxation, treats anxiety, fungal infections, allergies, depression, insomnia, eczema, nausea and menstrual cramps. Ylang-Ylang essential oil is anti-inflammatory, has a calming effect on the body, decreases blood pressure and heart rate and stops anxiety in its tracks. Clary Sage essential oil is a natural anti-depressant, used to reduce menopause symptoms and menstrual cramps. Lemongrass essential oil is used for pain relief, blood sugar regulation, improved digestion, stress and anxiety relief. Frankincense essential oil is also believed to be effective in fighting breast, prostate, pancreatic, skin, and colon cancer cells, preventing the spread of cancer cells, and reducing the side effects of cancer treatment. Orange essential oil is known for its ability to lift mood, reduce stress, treat skins conditions, reduce pain and inflammation, and relieve upset stomach, Myrrh essential oil kills harmful bacteria, supports mouth health. It is also a calming fragrance used to clean and treat wounds. Myrrh has anti-cancer benefits and is powerful fixative. Ginger: protects the skin against free radicals, includes over 40 antioxidant properties, safeguards the skin from premature ageing, improves elasticity and rejuvenates the complexion. Peppermint essential oil is known to reduce pain, fight against headaches and muscle ache. As well as improve mental function, and reduce stress.

A Message From The Father About Expectation:

Dear Heart,

This is what the Father would have you to know about expectation. To expect is to believe Me. To believe My promises. To meet each day with excitement, confidence, and wonder. When you move in expectation, you jump out of bed with a pep in your step that overrides the sickness you feel in your body and ignores the aches you feel in your bones. Like a pregnant woman with a swollen belly, you move with the certainty that today is the day that my promised package from the Almighty will arrive; and that when it gets here, it's gonna be good. Really, really good. Out-of-this-world-good. Make-you-forget-about-the-pain-of-delay-good. It's going to exceed your wildest dreams. You thought you were believing God for something big, but when the mail carrier arrives with this package, it won't be able to fit inside your current door. That means you're going to have to relocate. You're going to have to change structures. Reevaluate your dwelling space. You are going to have to shift paradigms and adopt a growth mindset. You are going to have to expand in every possible way — physically, mentally, emotionally and spiritual in order to receive the promised blessing that the Lord your

God has for you.

When to Use this Oil

Use this oil as a follow up oil after you have anointed yourself for the appropriate number of days with the oil of release. If you are believing God for any promised thing— whether that be personal healing, deliverance for a wayward child, or systemic justice, stir up the gift of joy on the inside of you and anoint yourself with the Oil of Expect.

Who Should Use the Oil of Expectation:

The oils in this blend are known for their ability to increase memory, promote restful sleep, reduce brain fog and promote physical energy. Anoint yourself with the oil of expect if you are experiencing insomnia, brain fog, fear, or restlessness. Also use this oil if you are joyfully waiting on the promises of God.

Declaration For the Oil of Expect:

To expect is to command the blessing. When you command the blessing, all of Heaven begins to move as it pushes the promised destiny towards you. You, in turn, must move as well. Today, your declaration requires no words. Today you dance. Add a drop of the oil of expectation to clean palms. Cup hands over nose and mouth and breath in. Next, turn on some happy music and for the length of one song, dance.

When you are ready to sing a new song. Create a song and record the words in the space provided on the next page. Let it be a song that reminds you that God always keeps His promises. Let this song be your decree.

MY PERSONAL DECREE TO EXPECT

10

THE OIL OF CREATE

(Testimony, Law & Responsibility)

You will also declare a thing and it will be established for you; So light will shine on your ways.

Job 22:28

The Oil of Create

The Oil of Create is comprised of Bergamot essential oil, Geranium essential oil, Lavender essential oil and Hyssops essential oil in an Olive oil blend. Bergamot essential oil is known for its ability to reduce inflammation, lower cholesterol, increases positive mood, reduce stress and anxiety, and alleviate symptoms of depression. Geranium essential oil is known for its antimicrobial, antifungal and antiviral properties. It is also an affective aid against anxiety, depression and skin infections, as well as being a great oil for pain management. Lavender essential oil promotes relaxation, treats anxiety, fungal infections, allergies, depression, insomnia, eczema, nausea and menstrual cramps. Hyssop essential oil fights infection, purifies and alleviates asthma and respiratory symptoms.

A Message From The Father About Creation:

Dear One,

To create means to bring into existence, to design, to declare, to make. You are created in the image and likeness of the Almighty One. The King of Kings, The Lord of Lords. The Ancient of Days, the Lion of Judah, The Prince of Peace, the Holy One of Israel. The Great I AM. I spoke everything you see and everything you don't see into existence: galaxies, stars, suns, moons, planets, birds, fish, the seas—I spoke it all into existence. The only time I ever became intimately involved in the creation process was when I created you. Made in the image and likeness of Me, you are

My most cherished masterpiece. Each and every one of you, exquisite and unique in your design. I took dust from the ground, divinity from Myself and formed mankind. Then I breathed life into him. Everything else I spoke. In the very depths of your being, you possess My same creative power. You can create things with your mouth. The key is to draw nearer to Me, and to hear what I want to be created. To hear My will. In this season, I AM asking you to be like Me. There are some inner vows that you have made, some words spoken over you and through you that have brought about a curse. Now, in this season, I ask you to write a new law, create a new reality by hearing a sound from heaven and then declaring it. So as you anoint yourself this morning with the Oil of Create, go ahead and declare something new over your life. I give you permission to speak. Create something spectacular. Create something the world has never seen before. Create something that your family has never seen before, your nation, your people group, your tribe, has never seen before. Come up here to where I AM, learn from Me. I will teach you how to speak.

When to Use this Oil:

THE REALM OF DECLARATORY GRACE

Use the Oil of Create after you have walked through the process of anointing yourself with the nine other oils in the series. After you have used the Oil of Live, Stand, Thrive, Remember, Laughter, Return, after you Keep, Release, and Expect now, you are finally ready to Create.

Who Should Use The Oil Of Create:

Artists, creatives, prophets, parents, intercessors. People looking for the complete will of God to be performed in their lives.

Declaration For The Oil Of Create:

Here is where you write your own declaration. Go up to the high places, hear what God is saying is true about you, especially those things that have not manifested themselves yet in the earth. Write your declaration in the space provided and anoint yourself with the Oil of Create daily until you see every promised thing you declared manifested in the earth. Until you are ready to do that please feel free to utilize my personal declaration on the next page. Adlib or substitute where you need to.

A MODEL PERSONAL DECLARATION

I am blessed. My husband is blessed. My seed—blessed. My Family line—blessed. My thought life—blessed. My future—blessed. Everything and Everybody that I call mine is utterly, ubberly, and ridiculously blessed. I'm like the children of Israel- not the ones who died in the desert, but the New Breed who GREW, EVOLVED and INHERITED the land. All of their clothes, shoes and accessories, evolved too. Until I fully inherit the good land that God has given me, I decree that everything I have been given stewardship over will grow and evolve too. I declare complete immunity for all my possessions against the natural and unnatural forces of time, destruction and decay. My body is blessed. Even now my waistline is decreasing as I give birth to everything God has promised. My physical body is morphing, it is a symbol in the Earth. I have been pregnant with a very many things for a very long time. I am giving birth spiritually and I am shedding pounds naturally.

I live in the Land of No Regrets. I don't walk after the consul of the ungodly, nor do I stand in the way of the

THE REALM OF DECLARATORY GRACE

sinners, nor sit in the seat of the scornful. My delight is in the law of The Lord, and on His law I do meditate both day and night. Therefore, I take no consul from: should have, would have, or I wish I could have. I am connected to the right Heaven and the right Earth. I soar with eagles, and I take my consul from THE ONE who is greater than time. He told me to RUN! THIS is my time. THIS is my season. I am blooming where I have been planted and everything that THE LIVING GOD planted inside of me is prospering NOW. He put a sure Word in my belly, and that Word IS traveling throughout the whole earth NOW. There is no corner nor crevice, nor industry on this globe that that Word OF GOD that is on the inside of me shall not go. I publish His works throughout the earth and streams multiply in the desert NOW. Blind eyes OPEN NOW. Deaf ears UNPLUG NOW, because the Spirit of The Lord is upon me NOW. I am anointed to preach, to teach, to proclaim liberty to the captives, and to break out of prison all who have been bound. Today a law goes into effect, the Heavens and Earth witness this governmental shift. I am well within my legal rights, and jurisdiction to decree such a thing. Before the foundation of the world, God established my coast. Before He established the boundary lines of the seas, He determined what would be the scope of my authority. Before I was fashioned in my mother's womb He set me apart. He appointed me to be a prophet to the nations. It is my birthright to uproot, to tear down, to destroy, to overthrow, to build and to plant. I have a breaker anointing. I raise the dead. I live in a constant state of forgiveness for all who hurt, oppress me and offend me. And my debts both spiritually, naturally, and otherwise are forgiven. I have no tolerance for the spirit of the thief. On behalf of my family, my nation, my place in history, and every shared ethnic link, I decree and declare a seven-fold return of, all health, every gift, every penny, every acre of land, every anointing that has been stolen from me and my constituents NOW.I declare a supernatural increase into the kingdom now. This is the year that I recover all.

We've come to the end of the work section of our workbook. Now, when you are ready to do so, use the provided space to begin crafting your own personal declaration. Decree (speak) your declaration daily until everything in it comes to past. When everything God has shown you comes to past, look around your life and your world and see what else needs to be

THE REALM OF DECLARATORY GRACE

changed. Then go make some new laws.

MY PERSONAL DECLARATION

11

APPENDIX A

THE HISTORY OF BIBLICAL ANOINTING OILS & WHY WE SHOULD USE THEM TODAY

Is anyone among you sick? Let them call the elders of the church to pray over them and anoint them with oil in the name of the Lord. And the prayer offered in faith will make the sick person well; the Lord will raise them up. If they have sinned, they will be forgiven. Therefore, confess your sins to each other and pray for each other so that you may be healed. The prayer of a righteous person is powerful and effective.

James 5:14-16

Why We Should Use Anointing Oils Today

The word anointing actually means to smear with oil or ointment. In Biblical days, it was fully understood that when the scripture in James 5 says, "let the sick call for the elders to anoint them with oil and pray over them," that the oil the elders used would not just be vegetable oil. Everyone understood that the oil being used was a combination of natural healing plants infused into a carrier oil such as olive oil which was plenteously available in that region of the world.

The elder's prayer of faith and the healing aromatic components of the oils worked together in synergy to heal the individual coming for prayer. Because antibiotics had not yet been discovered at the time, all people groups of the Earth relied on aromatic plants and prayers to whatever deity they served to heal themselves. The people of God just had the wisdom to know that there is only one prayer of faith that can heal, that's the one prayed to Jehovah Rapha, our Healer.

THE REALM OF DECLARATORY GRACE

AROMATHERAPY IN THE BIBLE

The Bible refers to essential oils or aromatic plants over 1000 times. In fact, God is the first aromatherapist. In Exodus chapter 30, God gives Moses the recipe for the holy anointing oil that would be used to anoint the priest and all the instruments used in the tabernacle.

Essential oils are very expensive now and they were very expensive in Biblical days. Because of the extremely high cost of aromatic plant oils, essential oils were only used by royalty and the very wealthiest people in society. So when the wise men presented the Baby Jesus, with Frankincense and Myrrh (both considered the most valuable of all essential oils for both their aroma and healing properties) they were recognizing Jesus's Sovereign Lordship. In Biblical days these two oils would only be found in royal palaces.

The healing properties of essential oils were legendary. No one had to tell their users how to apply them. For example, Mary would have known that she could rub Myrrh on her belly to heal her stretch marks and that the scent of the oil would be calming and comforting to her infant child when she nursed him. Also no one would have had to tell her to use Frankincense to protect her baby both from natural predators like viruses and from supernatural predators like demons, because the people of that time period understood the aromatic properties of the plant would ward these enemies off.

The Old Testament priest also practiced aromatherapy. Leviticus chapter fourteen tells us that the priest would apply oil to the right tip of the earlobe of the one being cleansed, on the thumb of his right hand, and on the big toe of his right foot—all points on the body where aromatic oils could be easily absorbed into the bloodstream.

Mary of Bethany anointed Jesus with Spikenard. She anointed His head and his feet. Jesus said she did this to prepare Him for his death and burial. Many of the components within Spikenard have the ability to heal old wounds. The oil also carries along with it the ability to prepare a person spiritually, mentally and emotionally for a difficult challenge. How beautiful for the Father to inspire Mary to do this for our Lord right before He would endure the greatest fight of His natural life.

THE REALM OF DECLARATORY GRACE

ABBA'S EARTH ANOINTING OILS

If you have experienced my ministry, you know that oftentimes I minister with oils. What most people don't know is that those oils are all blends that the Father gave me.

I discovered the healing ministry of aromatherapy and essential oils during my college years. At the time, I began to study everything I could about the healing nature of plants and their effects on the body.

One day, I received a box shipped to my home by mail by a very reputable company that I had often ordered from in the past. The box contained an array of precious very costly essential oils. I knew that there was no way I could afford the oils in that box and that there had to have been a mistake. Even still, I couldn't help opening the box and smelling the precious bottles within. I called the company because the box contained several hundreds of dollars' worth of oil and I didn't want to receive a bill. I was told by the company to keep the oils as a gift. I am convinced that the gift came from the Father who wanted me to learn how to use these wonderful oils.

Today, all of Abba's Earth Anointing Oils are a blend of the finest, therapeutic grade essential oils mixed in a natural vegetable oil base. Each oil in our line has an accompanying scripture verse to pray and stand on as you use the oil. Always pray and ask God which oil you should use whenever praying and anointing yourself or others.

Whenever I am anointing myself or anyone else with Abba's Earth Anointing Oils, the first thing I do is dab a little bit of oil into the palm of my hand and cup my hands over my nose and breathe deeply. I do this because the molecules in essential oils are small enough to past the blood brain barrier. When we breathe them in, they go directly into the bloodstream and heal the way they are sent forth to do. Fragrance oils created in a laboratory by man cannot do this. Only the pure plant oils created by God the Father have the ability to heal.

You can order Abba's Earth oils by emailing: ironerspress@gmail.com

12

APPENDIX B

ABBA'S EARTH ANOINTING OILS

I have three different anointing oil lines. **The Declaratory Grace Collection**, **The Scared Temple Collection** and **The Fragrant Offering Collection.** Please see information about each Line below.

DECLARATORY GRACE COLLECTION

The oils in the Declaratory Grace line are made from a thoughtful blend of essential oils mixed in virgin olive oil. Each unique blend is one that I believe our Heavenly Father has given me. There are ten oils in this line. Each oil comes with a personal declaration and a Word from the Father regarding the oil. Each oil in The Declaratory Grace collection should be used daily for either 40 days or a time period agreed upon by you and God. A downloadable copy of my book, *The Realm of Declaratory Grace Workbook* is included for free when you purchase the entire set. **($20 each/ $200 for complete set)**

Oils in the Declaratory Grace line and the order they should be used in:

1. **Live** (unity)

2. **Stand** (Union, Division, Witness)

3. **Remember** (Resurrection, Divine completeness)

4. **Thrive** (Creation)

5. **Laughter** (Grace, God's goodness)

6. **Return** (Weakness of man, Manifestation of sin)

7. **Keep** (Completion, Spiritual perfection)

8. **Release** (New beginnings)

9. **Expect** (Fruit of the Spirit)

10. **Create** (Testimony, Law and Responsibility)

THE SCARED TEMPLE COLLECTION

The Scared Temple Collection is the first line of essential oil based anointing oils that The Father inspired me to create. There are 14 oils in this collection. At the leading of the Holy Spirit use them to anoint yourself and others. Below I have included key information about each oil. **(Each oil in The Scared Temple Collection is $15/ $200 for the entire set)**

1. **BEAUTY FOR ASHES:** Lavender, Rosemary, Cedar, & Thyme essential oils, jojoba oil. Use for recompense & recovery after spiritual and physical loss (particularly hair loss). Isaiah 61:1-3 *The Spirit of the Sovereign Lord is on me, because the Lord has anointed me to proclaim good news to the poor. He has sent me to bind up the brokenhearted, to proclaim freedom for the captives and release from darkness for the prisoners, 2 to proclaim the year of the Lord's favor and the day of vengeance of our God, to comfort all who mourn,3 and*

provide for those who grieve in Zion—to bestow on them a crown of beauty instead of ashes.

2. **BREAKER**: Essential oils of Peppermint, Tea Tree, Eucalyptus, Lavender Essential oil and Olive oil. Use to Breaker to fight against physical (viral infections), spiritual infirmities (generational curses, demonic attacks) Psalm 103: 1-4 *Bless the Lord, O my soul, and all that is within me, bless his holy name! Bless the Lord, O my soul, and forget not all his benefits, who forgives all your iniquity, who heals all your diseases, who redeems your life from the pit.*

3. **COURAGE**: Essential oils of Orange, Cloves, and Peppermint are used in this formulation. Orange fights against fear and anxiety while Peppermint soothes the stomach, and Cloves strengthen the heart. Deuteronomy 31:6 *Be strong and of good courage, do not fear nor be afraid of them; for the LORD your God, He is the One who goes with you. He will not leave you nor forsake you.*

4. **FIRE**: *I baptize you with water for repentance, but he who is coming after me is mightier than I, whose sandals I am not worthy to carry. He will baptize you with the Holy Spirit and fire.* Matthew 3:11: A blend

THE REALM OF DECLARATORY GRACE

of Clove, Cinnamon, Frankincense, Peppermint, Eucalyptus, Red Thyme and Cedarwood Essential oils and Extra Virgin Olive oil. **When to Use**: Use Fire to burn out physical and spiritual impurities.

5. INTIMACY: Spikenard, Lavender essential oil, olive oil. Spikenard is the precious and costly aromatic that Mary of Bethany used to anoint Christ's feet with. It regulates the heartbeat, kills staph infections, and wounds that will not heal. Use this pleasant aroma to draw you into the presence of God. Zephaniah 3:17 *the Lord your God is in your midst, a mighty one who will save, he will rejoice over you with gladness, he will quiet you by his love; he will exult over you with loud singing.*

6. JOY: Orange, Grapefruit, Ylang–Ylang, and Myrrh essential oils and olive oil. The oils used in this blend are anti-depressant, antiseptic, useful for insomnia, nervous depression, anger and rage. Use the oil of Joy to fight against heaviness of heart, and for intercessors who have trouble dis-spanning spiritual burdens. **Psalms 5:11-12** *But let all who take refuge in you rejoice; let them ever sing for joy, and spread your protection over them, that those who love your name may* *exult in you. For you bless the righteous, O LORD; you cover him with favor as with a shield.*

7. **PEACE**: *The LORD make his face shine upon you and be gracious to you; the LORD turn his face toward you and give you peace."* Numbers 6:25-26 Lavender, Patchouli, Ylang-Ylang, and Myrrh essential oils and Extra Virgin Olive Oil. The aromatic oils in this blend are soothing, antiseptic, and, in combination, they act as a mild nerve sedative and a natural anti-depressant. Use Peace to combat spiritual, physical, and emotional effects of fear, anxiety & depression.

8. **THE PRIESTHOOD**: Essential oils of Myrrh, Cassia, Cinnamon, Calamus and Olive oil. A replica of the oils used in the Exodus chapter 30. God gave this blend to Moses to anoint the priests and the scared articles used in service to God. God specified that this oil should never be poured on an 'ordinary' person but to be reserved for the priest. Since we are now a nation of kings and priest, we can use this blend. Use this blend anytime you are preparing to enter a time of intercession or worship. Let it be a sweet, fragrant offering to the Father as you minister before him. *22 Then the Lord said to Moses, 23 "Take the*

THE REALM OF DECLARATORY GRACE

following fine spices: 500 shekels of liquid myrrh, half as much (that is, 250 shekels) of fragrant cinnamon, 250 shekels of fragrant calamus, 24 500 shekels of cassia—all according to the sanctuary shekel—and a hin of olive oil. 25 Make these into a sacred anointing oil, a fragrant blend, the work of a perfumer. It will be the sacred anointing oil. 26 Then use it to anoint the tent of meeting, the ark of the covenant law, 27 the table and all its articles, the lampstand and its accessories, the altar of incense, 28 the altar of burnt offering and all its utensils, and the basin with its stand. 29 You shall consecrate them so they will be most holy, and whatever touches them will be holy. 30 Anoint Aaron and his sons and consecrate them so they may serve me as priests."

9. PROTECTION: A blend of Frankincense and Myrrh in Extra Virgin Olive Oil carrier base. When used together, Frankincense and Myrrh combine their strengths to become: antiseptic, anti-fungal, anti-inflammatory, and anti-depressant. These oils are oxygenating to the body tissues and support the immune system by enhancing the body's natural defense. Helpful in combat against fear, stress, and frustration. Use this oil when praying a prayer covering for physical, mental, emotional and or spiritual protection. The scripture verse for Protection is Psalm 91:1-8: *Whoever dwells in the shelter of the Most High will rest in the shadow of the Almighty. 2 I will say of the Lord, "He is my refuge and my fortress, my God, in whom I trust. 3 Surely he will save you from the fowler's snare and from the deadly pestilence. 4 He will cover you with his feathers and under his wings you will find refuge; his faithfulness will be your shield and rampart. 5 You will not fear the terror of night, nor the arrow that flies by day, 6 nor the pestilence that stalks in the darkness, nor the plague that destroys at midday. 7 A thousand may fall at your side, ten thousand at your right hand, but it will not come near you. 8 You will only observe with your eyes and see the punishment of the wicked."*

10. WOUNDS: A blend of Spikenard, Hyssops, Frankincense, Cassia, and Cedar essential oils. Use to heal physical as well as spiritual brokenness, particularly childhood wounds. Psalm 147:3 *He heals the brokenhearted and binds up their wounds.*

11. HEIGHTS: *The Lord God is my strength, And He has made my feet like hinds' feet, And makes me walk on my high places. Habakkuk 3:19* Heights, the

THE REALM OF DECLARATORY GRACE

oil of promotion. Anoint yourself with Heights when it is time to go to the next level in your spiritual walk. Anoint yourself with Heights when you need to change your perspective or elevation, when you need to push past all the noise and 'go up' in the Spirit to hear clearly from God. Heights is a blend of **peppermint, bergamot, vetiver, rosemary, geranium, and tea tree, essential oils in an olive oil base**. And because new levels often attract new devils, this blend combines oils that are antibacterial, anti-inflammatory, antispasmodic. Oils that work together to provide emotional, and spiritual balance and physical support for the entire body.

12. RIVERS: On the last day of the feast, the great day, Jesus stood up and cried out, "If anyone thirst, let him come to me and drink. Whoever believes in me, as the Scriptures have said, "Out of his heart will flow rivers of living water." Now this He said about the Spirit, whom those who believed in Him were to receive, for as yet the Spirit had not been given, because Jesus was not yet glorified. John 7:37-39. The oil of Rivers is made up of oils of essential oils of **ylang -ylang, cinnamon, and cardamon**, Bergamot, Blue Chamomile, Spearmint and Wintergreen.

If you have accepted Jesus Christ as your Lord and Savior, His promise to every believer is that His Holy Spirit who leads you into all truth will come and make His dwelling with you. When to use: Use Rivers to Anoint new believers who need the indwelling of the Holy Spirit, also use Rivers to anoint seasoned believers who need to stir up the gift of the Holy Spirit within. If you are unfulfilled, dissatisfied, living beneath your potential, or suffering from a hunger and thirst that only God can fill anoint yourself with Rivers.

13. TRAVAIL: *Before she travailed, she brought forth; Before her pain came, she gave birth to a boy. Who has heard of such a thing? Who has seen such things? Can a land be born in one day? Can a nation be brought forth all at once? As soon as Zion travailed, she also brought forth her sons. Isaiah 66:7-8* Travail is a deep form of prayer that transports the intercessor directly into the center of God's heart on a matter. The tears that come forth during this time of intercession are not born from natural feelings but spiritual ones. The intercessor feels and reacts to the heart of God. The oil of Travail- is made up of a combination of Clary Sage, Lavender, and Ginger essential oils inside of an olive oil blend. All oils that are powerful aids during the labor and delivery process. **When to Use**: anoint yourself or others with the oil of Travail when God wants to birth something quickly into the Earth. Use to oil of Travail so that the 'child' God wants birthed is not aborted, or deformed, but delivered safely and completely at the appointed time.

14. WAR CRY: *So the people shouted and the priest blew the trumpets; and when the people heard the sound of the trumpet, the people shouted with a great shout, and the wall fell down flat, so that the people went up into the city, every man straight ahead and they took the city.* Joshua 6:20 Both in times of spiritual warfare, and in times of high worship, it is fitting to release a battle or war cry. That sound is a signal to both the angelic army and your spiritual enemies. The sound means that a kinsmen redeemer/blood avenger has arisen and adorned themselves for battle. The warrior is coming to take back everything that was stolen from them and the people they represent. **When to Use**: Anoint yourself with War Cry at the Lord's leading when you are about to go into a time of personal or corporate intercession, when you need to collect the spoils of war for present, past and future generations. **Essential oils of clove, wintergreen, cedar, vetiver**

and are used in this blend. This blend is designed for respiratory health, stimulation of the brain, focus, and attention.

FRAGRANT OFFERING COLLECTION

My final oil line of anointing oils up is made from the most costly and precious essential oils our planet has to offer. These oils require a tremendous amount of fragrant plant matter in their production process. Literally millions of flower petals are taken through a natural distillation process, only to produce a small amount of oil. Both the purity and the scarcity of these oils drives up their price and market value and they are often used to create some of the most exquisite perfumes in the world. So why even offer something so rare and costly? Well, why not give such a beautiful, sacrificial gift to a King? This line was created for those who feel inspired to worship the Lord through scent. Anoint yourself with the oils in this line as a sign of surrender and worship before the King.

THE REALM OF DECLARATORY GRACE

Extravagant Worship (*$375) - Rose Otto in Jojoba oil base Rose Otto is a sweet floral essential oil known for it's ability to reduce depression and calm anxiousness. Rose Otto is also used to soothe inflammation, quiet muscular spasms, protect the body against viruses and promote youthful beauty and skin balance. Incidentally, I believe wholeheartedly that pure unabashed worship of our Lord and Savior can have the same bodily affect. Anoint yourself with Extravagant Worship in times of unabashed praise and thanksgiving and when you want to pour out your heart like rain before the Father. *Oh come, let us sing to the Lord; let us make a joyful noise to the rock of our salvation! 2 Let us come into his a great King above all gods. 4 In his hand are the depths of the earth; the heights of the mountains are his also. 5 The sea is his, for he made it, and his hands formed the dry land. 6 Oh come, let us worship and bow down ; let us kneel before the Lord, our Maker! 7 For he is our God, and we are the people of his pasture, and the sheep of his hand. Psalm 95:1-7*

Press: Most Holy Faith- (*$355) Sandalwood and Jasmine Essential oil in a jojoba oil base Jasmine is a floral essential oil with a musky scent. In aromatherapy, it's a widely accepted practice to apply Jasmine essential oil to the skin to lift mood, boost happiness, increase confidence and reduce anger, anxiety, and stress. Sandalwood is a woody scent used to settle the mind, promote peace, lower the blood pressure, detoxify the body, and improve memory. Use this oil in times of Pressing Prayer and Worship. *⁷ But whatever were gains to me I now consider loss for the sake of Christ. ⁸ What is more, I consider everything a loss because of the surpassing worth of knowing Christ Jesus my Lord, for whose sake I have lost all things. I consider them garbage, that I may gain Christ ⁹ and be found in him, not having a righteousness of my own that comes from the law, but that which is through faith in Christ—the righteousness that comes from God on the basis of faith. ¹⁰ I want to know Christ—yes, to know the power of his resurrection and participation in his sufferings, becoming like him in his death, ¹¹ and so, somehow, attaining to the resurrection from the dead. ¹² Not that I have already obtained all this, or have already arrived at my goal, but I press on to take hold of that for which Christ Jesus took hold of me. ¹³ Brothers and sisters, I do not consider myself yet to have taken hold of it. But one thing I do: Forgetting what is behind and straining toward what is ahead, ¹⁴ I press on to-*

THE REALM OF DECLARATORY GRACE

ward the goal to win the prize for which God has called me heavenward in Christ Jesus Philippians 3:7-14.

Head Lifter: The Sacrifice of Praise (*$275) St. John's wort and Frangipani essential oil in Jojoba oil base. Frangipani essential oil is a strong, exotic fragrance that enhances the mind and the body. Frangipani is also known to alleviate inflammation, headache, back pain and tinnitus. Frangipani is also a natural astringent and is used to strengthen the hair follicles and protect the scalp. Frangipani is also a calming fragrance used used to relieve stress and induce a sound sleep. St. John's Wort essential oil has a soft earthy smell that is mildly sweet. Therapeutically St. John's Wort is used to regenerate healthy cell growth, this oil is soothing to irritated skin, used for both pain relieve and the relief of heaviness and depression. This essential oil blends beautifully with Franginpani. *Lord, how are they increased that trouble me! Many are they that rise up against me.[2] Many there be which say of my soul, There is no help for him in God. Selah.[3] But thou, O Lord, art a shield for me; my glory, and the lifter up of mine head.[4] I cried unto the Lord with my voice, and he heard me out of his holy hill. Selah.[5] I laid me down and slept; I awaked;*

for the Lord sustained me.⁶ I will not be afraid of ten thousands of people, that have set themselves against me round about.⁷ Arise, O Lord; save me, O my God: for thou hast smitten all mine enemies upon the cheek bone; thou hast broken the teeth of the ungodly.⁸ Salvation belongeth unto the Lord: thy blessing is upon thy people. Selah. Psalm 3 KJV.

*Prices in the Fragrant Offering line represent current market rates. Based on growing seasons and current market conditions, rates are subject to change. Call for most updated pricing contact: ironerspress@gmail.com

ABOUT AUTHOR

ABOUT THE AUTHOR

Catrina J. Sparkman is a licensed, ordained minister and the founder of The Ironer's Press Ministries, which hosts Prayer Parties— a seasonal gathering of intercessors from all over the Midwest, as well as The Fourth Watch— a 3-6am prayer meeting, that happens every Friday morning in her home city. She is the author of various works of fiction and non-fiction. An inspirational speaker, consultant, presenter, and personal empowerment coach, for various churches and secular organizations, Catrina teaches on prayer, the prophetic ministry, healing and deliverance, and theatre arts. Mrs. Sparkman lives in Madison, WI with her husband, Wesley, and their three beautiful children. She can be reached at doingbusinesswithgod@gmail.com.

BOOKING INFO

To book Minster Sparkman for your next ministry event please contact: Kubernesis Administrative Services on behalf of the Ironer's Press. T: 858 663.7810 kubernesis.info@gmail.com

ALSO BY

Catrina J. Sparkman

Non-fiction:

Doing Buiness with God Series

Doing Business with God: An Everyday Guide to Prayer & Journaling

Intimacy the Beginning of Authority

Divine Revelation for a Twitter Generation: Growing in the Prophetic

Doing Battle With the Names of God

The Fourth Watch

THE REALM OF DECLARATORY GRACE

Intercession 101: The Heartbeat of God

Wired for War

<u>Fiction:</u>

Novels

Passing Through Waters

Opening the Floodgates

The Fire this Time

Plays

Mother Love

www.ingramcontent.com/pod-product-compliance
Lightning Source LLC
Chambersburg PA
CBHW030528080526
44586CB00011B/365